MY PET
GECKO

Rennay Craats

Weigl Publishers Inc.

Published by Weigl Publishers Inc.
350 5th Avenue, Suite 3304, PMB 6G
New York, NY 10118-0069
Website: www.weigl.com

Project Coordinator
Heather C. Hudak

Design and Layout
Terry Paulhus

Library of Congress Cataloging-in-Publication Data available upon request.
Fax 1-866-44-WEIGL for the attention of the Publishing Records department.

ISBN 978-1-60596-098-2 (hard cover)
ISBN 978-1-60596-099-9 (soft cover)

Printed in China
1 2 3 4 5 6 7 8 9 0   13 12 11 10 09

Photograph and Text Credits

Contents

What is a Gecko?

Geckos have interested people around the world for thousands of years. Each of these beautiful, colorful, and exotic lizards has a different personality. Gecko owners are provided with hours of amusement.

Like fish, geckos are best enjoyed from a distance. To keep a gecko healthy, do not handle him often.

Geckos are exciting to watch as they shed their skin, hunt for food, or climb around their surroundings. It is also fun to spy them hiding under leaves or between rocks.

Geckos are popular pets for both children and adults. Unlike cats and dogs, these creatures do not need to make regular visits to the **veterinarian**, be walked, or cuddled. Geckos require a pet owner who will love them and give them proper care. While caring for geckos is easier than caring for dogs or cats, having a gecko as a pet is still a big responsibility.

likeable lizards

- Geckos are one of the few lizard **species** that are completely harmless.
- Most lizards are very quiet, but geckos use their voices to attract mates and to scare off intruders. In fact, geckos were named for the chirping noise they make. Their chirping sounds like the word "gecko."

- Geckos can be found on every continent except for Antarctica. The weather in Antarctica is too cold for geckos to survive.
- The most popular type of pet gecko in North America is the leopard gecko. This type of gecko is the easiest to keep and breed in **captivity**.

Pet Profiles

There are hundreds of gecko species. While all geckos are part of the reptile **family**, each species behaves and looks different. Some are great climbers, while others stay close to the ground. Some are **nocturnal**, while others are active during the day. Some geckos have scales of solid colors, while others have exciting patterns.

Geckos are found all over the world. Of the more than 700 different gecko types, most are not kept as pets. Only some gecko types make good pet pals.

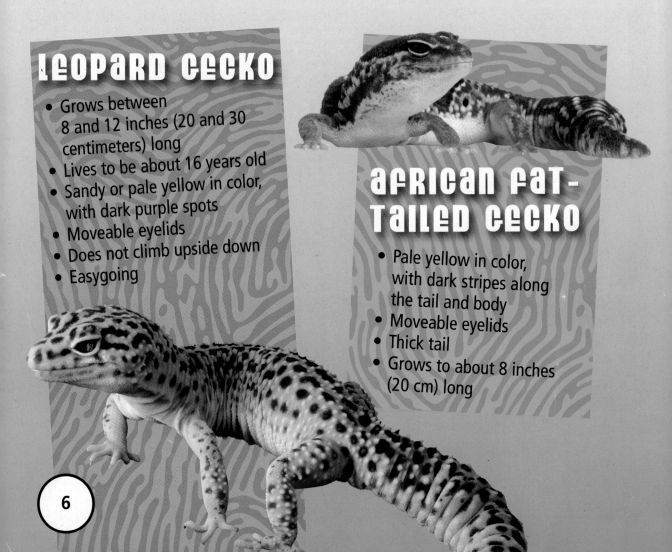

Leopard Gecko

- Grows between 8 and 12 inches (20 and 30 centimeters) long
- Lives to be about 16 years old
- Sandy or pale yellow in color, with dark purple spots
- Moveable eyelids
- Does not climb upside down
- Easygoing

African Fat-Tailed Gecko

- Pale yellow in color, with dark stripes along the tail and body
- Moveable eyelids
- Thick tail
- Grows to about 8 inches (20 cm) long

CRESTED GECKO

- Changes color
- Triangle-shaped head with crests, or ridges, along the back
- Grows between 7 and 8 inches (18 and 20 cm) long
- Easygoing
- Does not grow a new tail
- Lives between 10 and 15 years

BANDED GECKO

- Has a slim body with a thick tail
- Tan or yellow in color, with brown stripes across the body
- Small claws for climbing on rocks
- Grows between 4 and 6 inches (10 and 15 cm) long

TOKAY GECKO

- More aggressive than many other types of gecko
- One of the largest geckos, at about 14 inches (36 cm) long
- Pale blue or gray in color, dotted with orange spots
- Large eyes that bug out
- Climbs upside down
- Happiest living and hiding in trees

MADAGASCAR DAY GECKO

- Grows between 8 and 10 inches (20 and 25 cm) long
- Bluish-gray in color, with dark, large head
- Climbs well
- Active during the day
- Large eyes with round pupils

From Dinosaur to Docile

Geckos have been roaming Earth for a very long time. About 300 million years ago, reptiles, such as the gecko, **evolved** from amphibians. Reptiles are air-breathing animals that are covered with scales, such as turtles and snakes. Amphibians are cold-blooded animals, such as frogs and salamanders.

In Southeast Asia, the tokay gecko is thought to bring people good luck, good fortune, and many children.

During the **Mesozoic Era**, gecko-like lizards roamed nearly everywhere in the world. Geckos are strong reptiles. They survived when dinosaurs died. Geckos have not changed much since their early years on Earth. A gecko is more than just a pet—he is a close link to the age of dinosaurs.

Today, humans and geckos share the same living space. In warm climates, geckos sometimes streak across the ceiling or race up the walls of people's homes. In North America, people began keeping geckos as pets in the 1970s and 1980s. Many types of lizards became popular pets into the 1990s. As geckos became more popular, pet stores made more gecko species available for purchase.

Antique Art

- Geckos often appear in art, pottery, and jewelry from the Southwestern United States.
- Geckos can be a welcome addition to homes located in warm climates. These lizards eat bugs crawling around inside the house.
- In the 1950s, many American women wore pins shaped like anoles, or color-changing lizards.

Life Cycle

Young geckos look very similar to adult geckos. As some geckos grow older, their skin patterns and colors change. Whether a gecko is a few months old or many years old, he needs plenty of love and attention to stay happy and healthy.

Eggs

After geckos awake from **hibernation**, they breed. Between May and September, the female gecko lays eggs, usually two at a time. There may be as many as ten groups of eggs laid by one gecko each season. About 6 to 10 weeks later, the eggs hatch. By this time, the mother has usually left the area. A few days after the babies hatch, they are able to hunt and protect themselves from **predators**.

Hatchlings

At one week old, hatchlings shed their skin. Soon after, they begin to eat and live like adult geckos. Hatchlings look much like small adult geckos. They are often only a few inches long, depending on the species. Hatchlings' skin patterns and colors are bright and defined. The young geckos are often very energetic and excitable. They are fragile, and their skin is delicate for the first few months of their lives. Hatchlings can breed when they are about 10 months old.

Adult Geckos

By 18 months of age, most geckos have reached their full adult size. Adult geckos measure 8 to 10 inches (20 to 25 cm) from nose to tail and weigh 1.5 to 2 pounds (0.7 to 0.9 kilograms).

Mature Geckos

As geckos age, their bright or dark colors fade, and the pattern on their skin tends to spread. Mature geckos are calmer than young geckos.

living life

- Temperature affects whether an egg will produce a male or female gecko. If the eggs are **incubated** at a higher temperature, the geckos will be male. If the temperature is lower, the geckos will be female.
- Some leopard geckos can live as pets for more than 25 years.
- Once hatched, baby geckos eat their shells. They also eat their shed skin.

Picking Your Pet

There are many factors involved in choosing the right gecko as a pet. Research will help answer common questions about buying a reptilian friend.

Like most baby animals, baby geckos are fragile and can become sick easily.

What Will a Gecko Cost?

Not all pet stores sell these unusual animals. To find the right gecko, you may have to visit a reptile breeder or specialty store. Common geckos, such as the leopard gecko, cost less than rarer gecko species. When calculating the cost of owning a pet gecko, be sure to include the cost of the **terrarium**, food, and supplies. The terrarium and everything inside it, along with the animal itself, can cost hundreds of dollars. It is not very expensive to care for a gecko. Feeding a gecko is inexpensive since it only eats insects. Most geckos do not need to make regular trips to the veterinarian.

Do I Have Time for a Gecko?

Caring for a gecko does not take much time. Still, owners must set aside some time each day to care for their lizard. They should make sure the terrarium is the correct temperature and humidity. They also need to make sure the gecko has enough food and water, and the terrarium is clean. Owners must also make trips to the pet store to buy insects for gecko meals.

How Do I Choose the Right Gecko for Me?

A common species such as the leopard gecko will likely match a pet-seeker's needs. It is easy to care for these calm and easygoing lizards. Owners can carefully handle leopard geckos without being bitten. Some more aggressive species are known to bite when handled. Climate also determines which gecko species will make the best pet. For example, geckos that come from dry areas would not be suited to a hot, humid location.

Once Bitten...

- Always think about a pet's personality before buying it. The tokay gecko, for example, can be a cranky species. His bite can be serious and may even draw blood.
- Just one gecko of a rare species can cost several hundred dollars.

- When choosing a gecko, pet owners should consider whether the store or breeder gets the lizards from nature or breeds them in captivity. It is easier to care for geckos bred in captivity.

Gecko Gear

What you need to house a pet gecko depends on the species. Most gecko owners buy a terrarium to house their pet. Some gecko species are climbers. Taller terrariums work best for these species. Geckos who explore and hide on the ground require short, wide terrariums. Once the proper terrarium is in place, accessories can be added. Heat lamps shining over the terrarium help keep the correct temperature for these tropical animals.

To a gecko, hiding is not a game. If her tank does not have hiding places, she can become very ill or even die.

Some gecko species need humidity in their enclosures. Spraying water or placing tropical plants inside the enclosure is an easy way to keep moisture in the air. A water bowl is another important item.

Placing sand and plants inside the terrarium is a great way to copy a desert gecko's natural **habitat**. For other species, use bark made for reptile enclosures. **Mulch**, pea gravel, peat moss, or even paper towel often work well.

Decorating a gecko's terrarium is important and also fun. Pieces of wood, rocks, and plants make good hiding places. These items will help make your gecko feel comfortable and secure inside her enclosure.

Lizard Lair

- When decorating a gecko terrarium, avoid using materials found outside or around the house. Accessories need to be chemical-free so the gecko does not become sick.
- Depending on the species of your gecko and the location of her terrarium, a light may be a good addition to the enclosure. A light helps heat parts of the terrarium. It also creates a sense of day and night for the gecko.

- Never keep geckos of different species in the same terrarium. They will likely fight for their territory.
- Research how a species lives in nature. This will help determine what type of gecko is best for you.
- Some people place heat rocks in their gecko enclosure. This can be dangerous. If the gecko sits on the rock for too long, she can be burned.

Lizard Lunch

Geckos are not picky eaters, so feeding them is quite simple. They will eat nearly any insect that is small enough for them to swallow. All you need to do is either catch insects outdoors or purchase insects from a local pet store.

Geckos do not chew their food. They use their teeth to hold on to **prey**, and swallow insects whole.

Outdoor Food

Outdoor insects, such as cockroaches, grasshoppers, houseflies, and moths, are a delicious addition to a diet of store-bought insects. Before feeding outdoor insects to a gecko, make sure they have not been exposed to **pesticides**. Eating bugs sprayed with this poison can make the gecko sick.

Store-Bought Nutrition

Geckos like to eat crickets and mealworms. Crickets alone can be a great diet for a pet gecko, but your pet might enjoy some variety. Some mealworms and even fish-food flakes can make mealtime more exciting for a pet gecko, but be careful. Mealworm skin is hard for geckos to digest. Eating too many mealworms can cause health problems for geckos. Along with tasty insect treats, geckos need to take vitamins. Vitamin drops may be added to a gecko's water or brushed onto insects.

Gecko Grub

- It is difficult to know how much to feed a gecko. One sign that a gecko has had too much to eat are dead or dying insects inside his enclosure.
- It is a good idea to have a water bowl inside the gecko's enclosure. Even if the gecko does not drink from the bowl, live crickets placed inside the enclosure need the water to survive.

- Some gecko owners fatten up crickets before feeding them to their geckos.
- Some bigger gecko species enjoy eating newborn mice.
- Geckos born and raised in captivity may not eat outdoor insects. They may not realize a spider or grasshopper put in their enclosure is prey.

Lizard Looks

Different species of geckos have different **traits** and appearances. Still, all geckos share many similar features. These beautiful lizards are all covered with scales that are shed and replaced regularly. Unlike many other reptiles, geckos have strong senses of hearing, smell, and taste. This allows them to find food and detect predators.

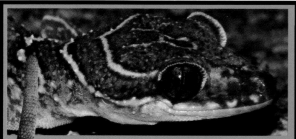

Most geckos have a triangular-shaped head that perches on their thick neck. Most other lizards have no neck at all—their heads connect directly to their bodies.

Geckos have long, wide tongues. The tongue detects particles in the air and places them on an organ inside the mouth called the Jacobson's organ.

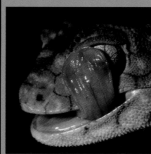

This organ helps geckos identify their surroundings. Geckos also use their tongues to keep their eyes clean.

Geckos have great night vision. During the day, the pupils of these nocturnal animals look like slits, but at night, the pupils **dilate** to nearly the size of the whole eye. Most geckos do not have eyelids. Instead, they have a clear **membrane** protecting their eyes.

If you hold some gecko species up to the light, you can see through their ears to the other side.

Geckos have better hearing than most other lizards. This comes in handy when geckos are hunting or communicating with one another.

Geckos are known for racing upside down on surfaces. Their feet allow them to climb nearly any surface. Many geckos have

hundreds of thousands of fine hairs on the bottoms of their feet. These tiny hairs, called spatulae, act as suction cups to grab hold of a surface and keep the gecko from falling or slipping.

Gecko tails are thin close to the body, wide in the middle, and thin again at the tip. Their tails store fat energy to keep them strong when there is not much food. Geckos can shed their tails. Their tails come away from their bodies and wiggle in front of predators. This gives geckos time to get away. It takes about one month for the tail to regrow.

Hands Off

Geckos are not furry, cuddly pets. They do not need to be brushed or petted. Some species are best left alone, while others can be picked up and handled with care. Sometimes, handling a gecko is necessary. The best way to pick up a gecko is to direct her into a plastic container. This will make it easier for you to clean out her terrarium.

Another way to pick up a gecko is to slip one hand under the lizard and use the other hand to gently hold her head. This must be done carefully so she does not feel threatened or bite. Some calmer species will walk onto their owner's hand for easy holding and moving.

Holding a gecko can cause her injury if you are not careful. When a gecko feels threatened, she will shed her tail to distract the source of that threat, even if that threat is her owner. Although the tail sometimes grows back, it causes the gecko stress. Losing a tail is not good for the gecko's health.

Handling a gecko can also cause her skin to tear. A gecko's skin is extremely delicate, especially when she is very young. She loses the top layer of skin naturally every few weeks.

Skin Deep

- While cats and dogs lick their fur to groom, geckos step out of their skin. Geckos shed their skin completely in a matter of several hours.

- Picking up and handling a gecko too often may cause her stress. This stress can lead to illness.

Healthy and Happy

Geckos do not get sick often. A healthy environment leads to a healthy pet. A clean enclosure free of sharp objects is a good start toward preventing illness and injury. Even the decorations inside the terrarium should be cleaned once a month. Cleaning rids them of any bacteria that could endanger the gecko.

Geckos can be treated with some of the same medicated creams used on people. Ask a veterinarian before using any product on a pet.

A healthy environment must have the proper temperature and humidity. Keeping a thermometer and **hygrometer** in the terrarium will ensure the gecko has healthy living conditions. A good diet is key for keeping your pet healthy.

Sometimes, geckos get sick. Owners can spot health problems by paying close attention to the behavior and appearance of their gecko. A change in the gecko's personality may be caused by a health problem. Some minor problems, such as ticks or mites, can be treated at home. There is a great deal of information about how to rid geckos of these pests. Simple store-bought treatments or even alcohol and tweezers can work. For more serious injuries or illnesses, geckos should visit a veterinarian who specializes in exotic animals or reptiles.

Inside Out

- Health problems occur more often in geckos born in nature than those born in captivity. Wild geckos can pass illnesses to captive ones.
- A lack of appetite, sluggish behavior, and diarrhea are all signs that a gecko could be suffering from an internal **parasite**. Geckos with an internal parasite must be treated by a veterinarian.

Lizard Behavior

Geckos, like other animals, have personalities. One gecko may be energetic and pounce on his dinner. Another might be slow-moving and relaxed. Despite these differences, geckos share many of the same behaviors.

Geckos hide when they sleep. This protects them from predators. Be sure to have plenty of hiding places in the terrarium.

Geckos do not hunt for food. This does not mean they are poor hunters. If a gecko is hungry and spots an insect nearby, he will stalk it like a lion stalks prey. He never takes his eyes off the insect. Then, in the blink of an eye, the gecko snaps up his meal with his tongue and licks his lips.

Geckos often shed their skin. When it is time to **molt**, geckos will slow down. They do not climb or walk as much as usual. As the skin begins to loosen from the gecko's body, he will tug at it to help the process along. He will also eat the skin for extra nutrition. Sometimes, molting is not complete, and there are patches of skin left on tough areas, such as the feet. Geckos will yank on these skin patches much like a cat or dog would work to get leaves or tree sap out of their fur.

Pet Peeves

Geckos do not like:
- loud noises
- being handled
- too much attention
- having their tails pulled

lizard lessons

- Geckos are very **territorial**. They may become violent if their territory is threatened.
- Female geckos of some species can reproduce without a male gecko. The result is a **clone** of the mother.

- Most gecko mothers lay eggs and then leave. Some, such as the tokay gecko, guard the eggs. Both the father and mother have been known to fight other geckos that get too close to the nest.

Gecko Tales

People have written about geckos for centuries. These prehistoric lizards are an important part of some cultures' **mythology**. In Hawai'i, geckos are thought to represent a magical lizard called the mo'o. Hawai'ian peoples, known as Polynesians, also believed that the mo'o could turn into a gecko. Geckos are respected and cherished in Polynesian society.

How the Gecko Got His Voice

Once upon a time, there lived a very rich and greedy man named Gecko. His life was filled with pleasure. One day, Gecko met the queen's brother Vuong. It was believed that Vuong was as rich as Gecko. Gecko did not believe this, so he challenged Vuong to a contest. The two men would allow their homes to be judged. The judges would decide which of the two men had more riches. The winner would take over the other man's home. After hours of looking at the many jewels and treasures of each home, the judges could not decide. Vuong thought of a new challenge. Gecko's house was filled with many riches, but he did not have some of the common items found in a house. Vuong asked Gecko to show him a used clay cooking pot. Gecko did not own a clay pot. As promised, Gecko gave his home to Vuong. For miles around, people could hear Gecko sighing and clucking his tongue over his loss. When he died, Gecko was turned into a small lizard.

From *VietnamStyle's* "The Gecko's Tale."

Geckos have found their way into paintings, artistic photographs, sculptures, clothing, and jewelry. Their unique colors and patterns, as well as their unusual body shapes, have inspired many artists. Geckos are also thought to bring luck. Wearing jewelry or displaying art with a gecko image has become popular. Some companies are using the gecko name or image to promote their business.

Lizard Lore

- Polynesians believe that, if you destroy a gecko egg, you will fall over a cliff.
- In Greek mythology, a goddess named Demeter turned a man into a gecko for laughing at her.
- American Indians of the Southwest United States believe the banded gecko of North America is a symbol of good luck. They often use the gecko image in artwork.

Pet Puzzlers

What do you know about geckos? If you can answer the following questions correctly, you may be ready to own a pet gecko.

Q Why are hiding places important for geckos?

A Geckos need to feel safe and secure. Without hiding places, they may become stressed, ill, or even die.

Q How do geckos stick to smooth, vertical surfaces?

A Tiny hairs on their feet act like suction cups to grip onto slippery surfaces.

Q Why is it harmful to handle a gecko too often?

A Geckos can feel threatened or stressed if they are handled too often. This can cause them to shed their tails. Holding a gecko can also damage his fragile skin.

Q What do geckos like to eat?

A Geckos like to eat crickets and mealworms. They will also eat outdoor insects, including cockroaches, flies, and grasshoppers.

Q How did the gecko get his name?

A Geckos are one of the only lizards to use their voices. Their chirping noise sounds like the word "gecko."

Q How many different types of geckos are there?

A There are more than 700 kinds of geckos.

Q What is unusual about baby geckos?

A After birth, baby geckos are usually left alone. When they hatch, they have to hunt and protect themselves without any help from their parents.

Getting a Gecko

Before you buy your pet gecko, write down some gecko names you like. Some names may work better for a female gecko. Others may suit a male gecko. Here are just a few suggestions.

Yoda

Lizzy

Spot

Buddy

Dino   Scaly   Digger   Rex

Gary   Lily

Frequently Asked Questions

Is it safe to have geckos in a house with other animals?

It is fine to have different kinds of pets in one house. You must make sure the gecko is protected from other animals. Never allow cats or dogs to be near your gecko enclosure without supervision. Also, a dog or cat staring in the terrarium can cause your gecko stress.

Are geckos an endangered species?

Only four species of gecko are endangered. Almost fifty gecko species are considered threatened. These animals are in trouble because their habitat is being destroyed. The numbers of some species are falling because of careless pet collectors.

Why is my gecko turning gray? What should I do?

There is nothing to worry about if your gecko's color fades or turns gray. This is a sign that she is shedding her skin. Allow your gecko to go through the process on her own. If she has trouble with the difficult areas, such as around the toes, you can help her out with a cotton swab dipped in hydrogen peroxide.

More Information

Animal Organizations

You can help geckos stay happy and healthy by learning more about them. Many organizations are dedicated to teaching people how to care for and protect their pet pals. For more gecko information, write to the following organizations.

Global Gecko Association

1155 Cameron Cove Circle
Leeds, AL 35094

Association for Reptilian and Amphibian Veterinarians

810 East 10th, P.O. Box 1897
Lawrence, KS 66044

Websites

To answer more of your gecko questions, go online, and surf to the following websites.

Gecko Care

www.geckocare.net

BBC: Tokay Gecko

www.bbc.co.uk/nature/wildfacts/factfiles/476.shtml

Leopard Gecko

www.leopardgeckocare.net

Words to Know

captivity: an animal kept in an enclosure

clone: an exact copy

dilate: to become larger

evolved: developed

family: related plants or animals

habitat: natural environment of an animal or plant

hibernation: a state of deep sleep that lasts throughout the winter months

hygrometer: an instrument used to measure humidity

incubated: kept warm until hatching

membrane: thin layer of tissue

Mesozoic Era: historical time period between 248 and 65 million years ago

molt: to make room for new growth by shedding feathers, hair, or skin

mulch: an item, such as straw or plastic sheeting, that is spread on the ground

mythology: an ancient set of stories that explain the history of a group of people

nocturnal: active at night

parasite: an organism that lives on or in other organisms to obtain nutrients

pesticides: chemicals used to kill insects

predators: animals that hunt and kill other animals for food

prey: animals that are hunted and eaten by other animals

species: a group of related animals

terrarium: glass tank with a screen lid

territorial: defending one's surroundings from outsiders

traits: distinct features of one's appearance or personality

veterinarian: animal doctor

Index